LAUGH LINES ARE BEAUTIFUL

Also by Leigh Anne Jasheway-Bryant

NOT GUILTY BY REASON OF MENOPAUSE

LEIGH ANNE JASHEWAY-BRYANT

LAUGH LINES ARE BEAUTIFUL

AND OTHER AGE-DEFYING TRUTHS

CELESTIAL ARTS

BERKELEY

Now that you're a "mature" woman,
you're smart enough to know . . .

If you were going to turn into your mother,
you would have done it by now.

Nothing makes you look firmer and less wrinkled than walking a Sharpei.

When your hair starts to get kinky,
your sex life should too.

You still look twenty-something.

From the back.

At night.

In the fog.

IF YOU WEAR *heels* AND *pearls* TO DO HOUSEWORK, YOU NEED YOUR MEDS ADJUSTED.

It's silly to long for a
washboard stomach
when you have
a dashboard stomach—
soft and padded,
with a built-in air bag.

Mood swings are a great excuse for getting people at work to leave you alone.

Superwoman undoubtedly does drugs.

The less perky your breasts,
the more quickly men pay attention
to what you have to say.

If it's a choice between staying in a bad marriage and re-entering the dating world,

get a dog.

A couple of glasses of wine are good for your heart.

A couple more glasses are good for your FANTASY LIFE.

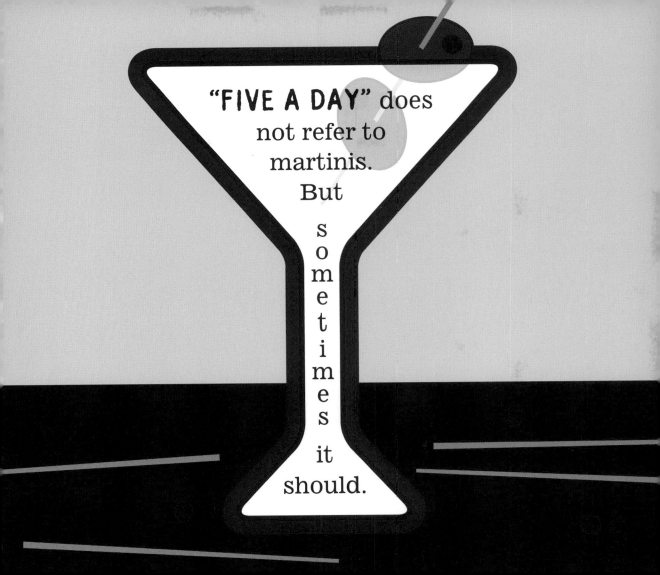

Your body shaper is too tight if you require CPR.

How important it is to spice up your sex life
by making love in exotic locations.

Like the other side of the bed.

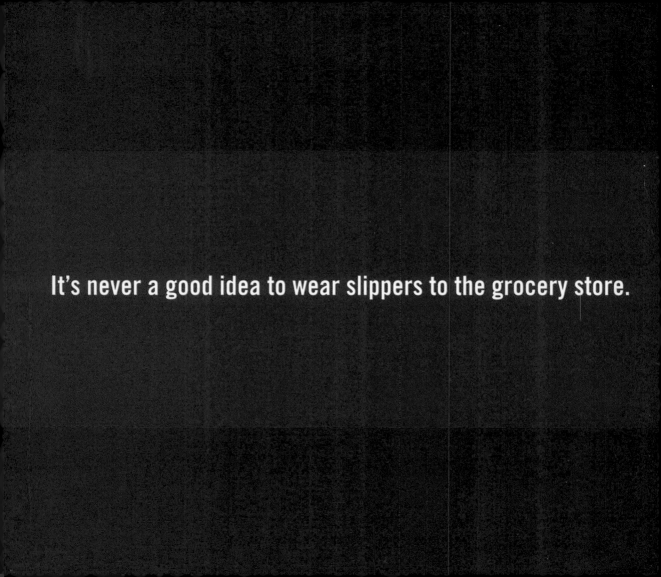

It's never a good idea to wear slippers to the grocery store.

Black may be slimming,

but chartreuse blinds and confuses people.

When to take no prisoners . . .

and when to use your
faux fur-lined
handcuffs.

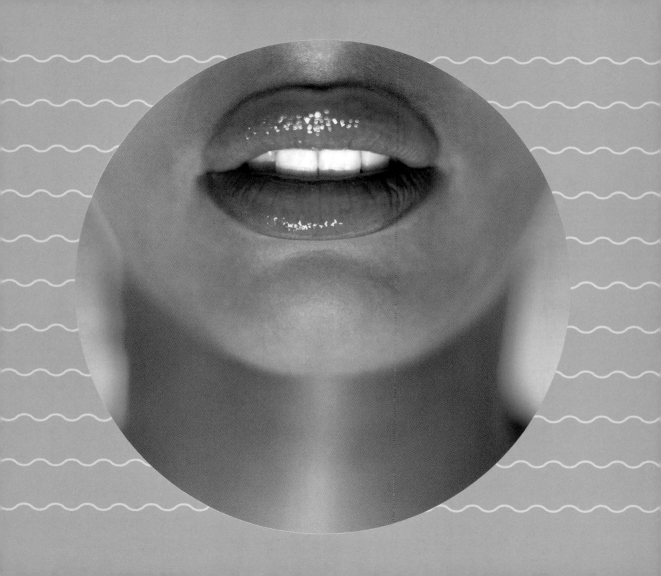

YOU'VE OVERDONE THE
COLLAGEN
IF YOUR LIPS ARE MISTAKEN FOR A
LIFE RAFT.

There are worse things than being the crazy cat lady.

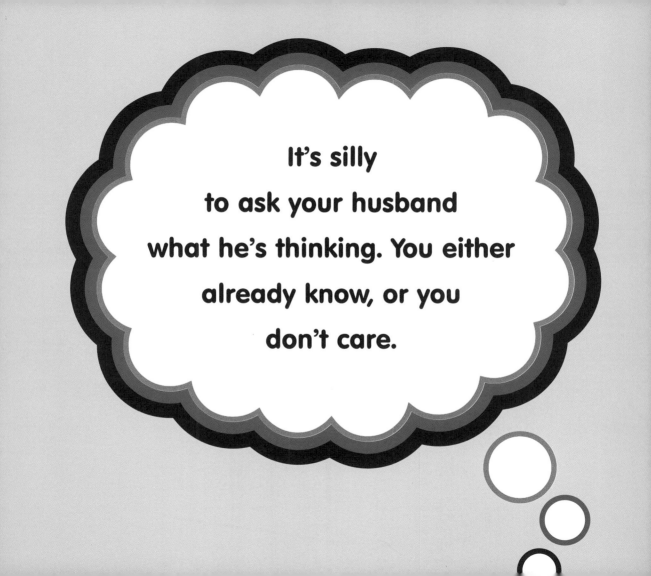

If you catch your husband reading a *Penthouse* magazine without his bifocals,

you have nothing to worry about.

"Book club" is code for
"Drinking with the girls."

Your butt is not your problem.

It's the problem of the person standing behind you.

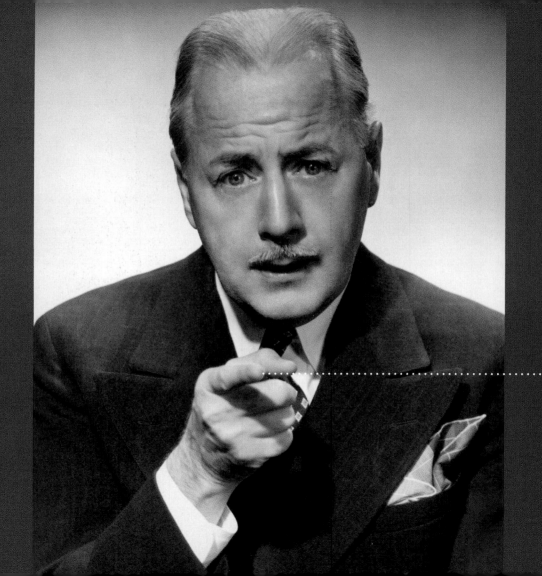

Even men with graying hair still think fart jokes are funny.

When it comes to leaving yourself notes on the bathroom mirror, red lipstick is a good choice.

DON'T FORGET
PANTIES!

It's best to think of your mammogram as your opportunity to pose topless for the camera.

Idle hands

call the Home Shopping Network.

Bald guys try harder.

The best form
of birth control is
whispering the words
"you're the daddy"
in your lover's ear.

IT'S STUPID TO HOLD IN YOUR
STOMACH AND YOUR **OPINIONS**
FOR ANYONE.

Wearing knee-highs **does not**

make you look younger.

A good man is hard to find in a bar at 3 A.M.

THE BEST TATTOOS ARE
THE ONES THAT REMIND YOU
OF SOMETHING IMPORTANT,
LIKE YOUR
KID'S BIRTHDAY.

If you don't get in trouble regularly, you're not

having enough **fun.**

The Kama Sutra

was written by a chiropractor

who needed more business.

At least you won't die by virgin sacrifice.

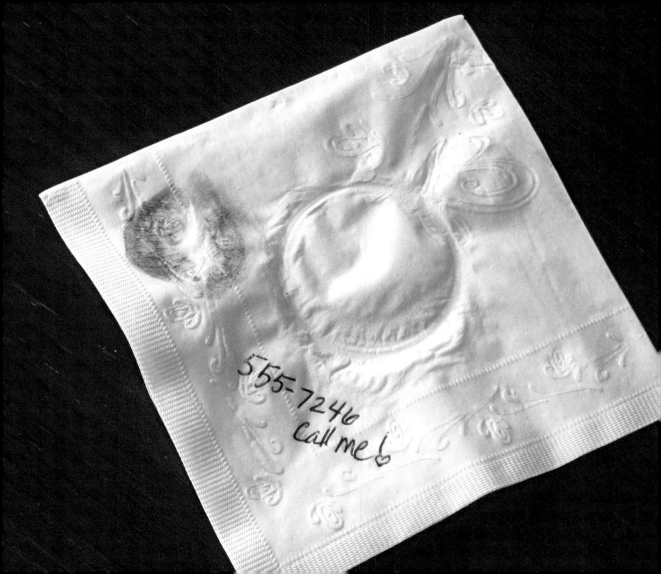

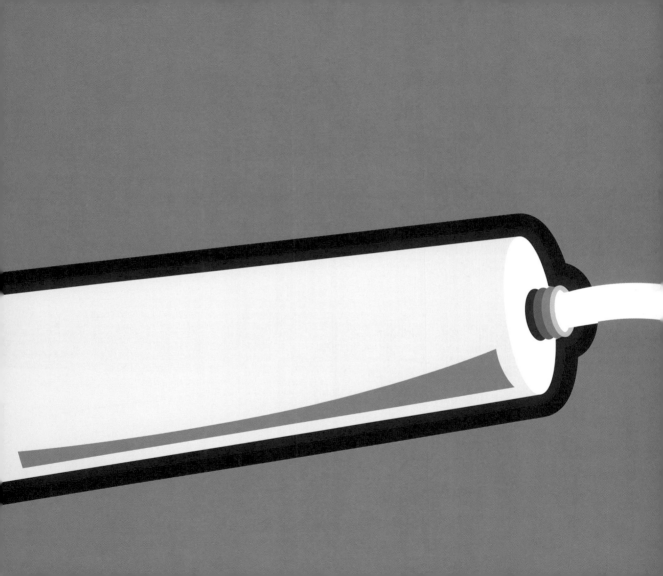

You should never
spend more on anti-aging creams
than you do on airline tickets.

Girlfriends are cheaper than therapy.

Giving someone the finger
looks classier when your nails are

MANICURED.

How to use duct tape as an emergency facelift.

Everything should be done in moderation.

Including moderation.

"Make mine a double"
may now refer to your chin.

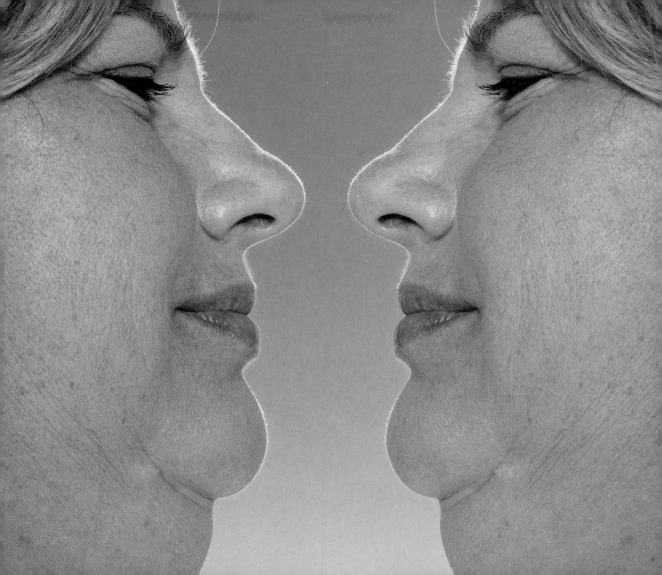

It *is* possible to be too thin,
too tan, and too bitchy.

It's easier to follow your bliss if you can see where you're going.

If you can't wiggle your toes, you've had too much Botox.

You should never send an

email after a night out with the girls.

A pogo stick is not a transportation option.

Elevator sex rarely lives up to its reputation.

Perimenopause is from the Greek, meaning **"partly homicidal."**

You're only half as old as your
mother was at your age.

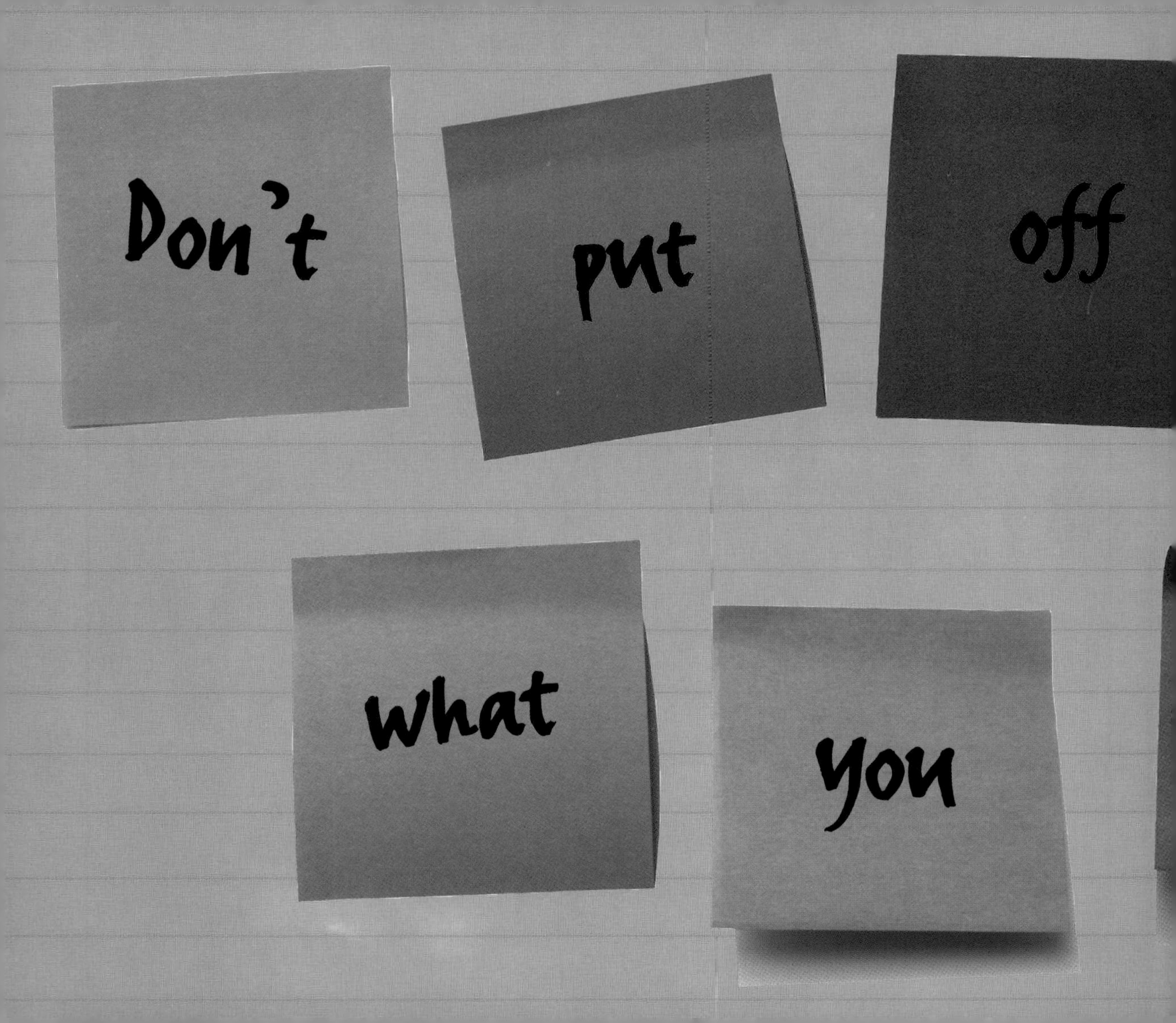
Don't
put
off
what
you

until tomorrow

still remember today.

How to win an argument

simply by raising an eyebrow.

Laugh lines are beautiful!

Published in the United States by Celestial Arts, an imprint of the Crown Publishing Group, a division of Random House, Inc., New York.
www.crownpublishing.com
www.tenspeed.com

Celestial Arts and the Celestial Arts colophon are registered trademarks of Random House, Inc.

Library of Congress Cataloging-in-Publication Data
Jasheway-Bryant, Leigh Anne.
  Laugh lines are beautiful : and other age-defying truths / Leigh Anne Jasheway-Bryant.
    p. cm.
  Summary: "More than 50 humorous one-liners about midlife paired with colorful graphics and vintage photographs"—Provided by publisher.
  ISBN-13: 978-1-58761-314-2
  ISBN-10: 1-58761-314-X
  1. Middle age—Humor. 2. Aging—Humor. I. Title.

PN6231.M47J37 2009
818'.602—dc22

2009008450

ISBN 978-1-58761-341-2

Printed in Singapore

Design by Betsy Stromberg

10 9 8 7 6 5 4 3 2 1

First Edition

Photographs on front cover (clockwise from top left) by Jack Hollingsworth / Getty Images/MedioImages; Getty Images/Photodisc; Pete Saloutos / Getty Images/ Photographer's Choice RF; Getty Images/Johner RF; James Steidl James Group Studios Inc. © istockphoto.com; Teri Dixon / Getty Images/Photodisc.

Photograph on page 4 by Teri Dixon / Getty Images/Photodisc.

Photograph on page 7 by Stacy Barnett / Shutterstock Images LLC.

Photograph on page 8 by Getty Images/Photodisc.

Photograph on page 11 by Perov Stanislav / Shutterstock Images LLC.

Illustrations on pages 12–13, 20, 28–29, 36–37, 44–45, 53, 68–69, 76–77, 100–101 by Betsy Stromberg.

Photograph on page 15 by Joop Snijder Jr. / Shutterstock Images LLC.

Photograph on page 16 by iofoto / Shutterstock Images LLC.

Photograph on pages 18–19 by Alloy Photography © Veer Incorporated.

Photograph on page 23 by John Lund/Paula Zacharias / Getty Images/Blend Images.

Photographs on pages 24, 46, 50, 54, 61, 102, 108–109 by George Marks / Getty Images/Retrofile.

Photograph on page 27 by Mark Coffey © istockphoto.com.

Photograph on page 31 by Getty Images / Image Source.

Photograph on page 32 by Stockbyte / Getty Images/Retrofile RF.

Photograph on page 35 by Getty Images/Blend Images.

Photographs on pages 38–39 by sofist © istockphoto.com.

Photograph on page 40 by Sydney Shaffer / Getty Images/Digital Vision.

Photograph on page 43 by Nicola Hackl-Haslinger © istockphoto.com.

Photograph on pages 48–49 by Angelika Schwarz © istockphoto.com.

Photograph on page 56 by James Steidl James Group Studios Inc. © istockphoto.com.

Photograph on page 58 by Getty Images/Stockbyte.

Photograph on page 62 by John Shepherd © istockphoto.com.

Photograph on page 65 by haveseen © istockphoto.com.

Photograph on page 67 by Ryan Lane © istockphoto.com.

Photograph on page 70–71 by Arthur Selbach / Getty Images/Westend61.

Photograph on page 72 by Michael Blann / Getty Images/Digital Vision.

Photograph on page 75 by Rebecca Ellis © istockphoto.com.

Photograph on page 79 by Getty Images/Uppercut RF.

Photograph on pages 80–81 by Rich Yasick © istockphoto.com.

Photograph on page 83 by Dan Brandenburg © istockphoto.com.

Photograph on page 85 by thumb © istockphoto.com.

Photograph on page 86 by Getty Images/Foodcollection.

Photograph on page 89 by Fotosearch.

Photograph on page 90 by SW Productions / Getty Images/Photodisc Red.

Photographs on pages 92–93 by Milos Luzanin and Donald Gruener © istockphoto.com.

Photograph on page 95 by Getty Images / Ingram Publishing.

Photograph on page 96 by Jack Hollingsworth / Getty Images/MedioImages.

Photograph on page 98 by paparazzit / Shutterstock Images LLC.

Photograph on page 105 by Pete Saloutos / Getty Images/ Photographer's Choice RF.

Photograph on pages 106–107 by Rebecca Grabill © istockphoto.com.

Photograph on pages 110–111 by Getty Images/Johner RF.